HOLLYWOOD
HEAVIES

EDITED BY J.C. SUARÈS

THOMASSON-GRANT

Published by Thomasson-Grant, Inc.

Printed in Hong Kong.

ISBN 1-56566-057-9

00 99 98 97 96 95 94 5 4 3 2 1

Inquiries should be directed to:
Thomasson-Grant, Inc.
One Morton Drive, Suite 500
Charlottesville, Virginia 22903-6806
(804) 977-1780

Edward G. Robinson
LITTLE CAESAR, 1931

They are the Hollywood stars we love to hate. James Cagney and Edward G. Robinson. Lee Marvin and Jack Palance. Bette Davis and Joan Crawford. Meaner than mean, tougher than tough, these big-box-office guys and dolls, gangsters and molls have electrified the big screen for decades with their dastardly deeds and wicked ways.

For every dashing Hollywood hero there is an equally devious heavy waiting in the wings to bring the good guy to his knees. The bad guy may lose in the end, but Hollywood's best villains always manage to steal a few scenes, chew up the scenery, and spit out the best lines along the way.

Some of our favorite celluloid psychos and creeps have become so identified with their roles that their on-screen characters will live in infamy forever. James Cagney may have been a hoofer at heart, but he will always be Public Enemy Number One to us. Edward G. Robinson *is* Little Caesar, and Paul Muni, Scarface. Bette Davis may have played a variety of parts, but she was at her best being bad—staring down her dying husband in *Little Foxes* and her back-stabbing understudy in *All About Eve*. And Joan Crawford in her later roles was . . . well . . . Joan Crawford!

Not every heavy has a heart of stone, of course. Having started his career playing two-bit hoodlums and gangsters, Humphrey Bogart was the first (and best) of the heavies with a heart of gold—rough and tough, but human, too. And who didn't secretly admire Marlon Brando and Paul Muni in their "godfather" roles? They were devoted family men, after all.

Then there are the rare screen heavies who broke all the rules: Ernest Borgnine, Clint Eastwood, Lee Marvin, and Sylvester Stallone all began their acting careers as the vilest of villains. They reinvented them-selves, and today they are some of Hollywood's best-loved heroes.

In the end, the classic battle between good and evil is one that is waged on the screen as well as off. There is a little bit of the devil in all of us, and if we can't help but root for the bad guy now and then, at least we'll have some wicked good fun in the process.

Gert Frobe (with Sean Connery)
GOLDFINGER, 1964

*Although the German-born one-time violinist, stage designer,
and cabaret performer had appeared as a heavy in numerous
international films since the 1940s, he is best remembered for his
vicious turn as the gold-loving, power-mad villain who plans to
blow up Fort Knox in this third installment of the popular
James Bond spy-thriller series. Assisted by his outrageous henchmen,
Oddjob and Pussy Galore, Frobe's maniac-with-a-Midas-touch
is one of the big screen's most memorable meanies.*

Charles Laughton (with Clark Gable)
MUTINY ON THE BOUNTY, 1935
*Having already played a number of effective heavies in films
such as* The Private Life of Henry VIII *and* The Barretts of
Wimpole Street, *the Oscar-winning English-born character actor
gave such a convincing portrayal of the notorious Captain Bligh,
he soon felt obliged to leave Hollywood in order to escape
further typecasting. The husband of sometime-screen-villainess
Elsa Lanchester* (The Bride of Frankenstein) *eventually
returned to Tinseltown to star as a heavy again—
albeit one with a heart of gold—in his second-most-famous role,
as the title character in* The Hunchback of Notre Dame.

Bette Davis

THE LITTLE FOXES, 1941

Looks <u>do</u> kill when Warner Bros.' temperamental superstar stares
down her dying husband in this screen version of the Lillian Hellman
play about a vituperative Southern woman motivated by power
and greed. Commenting about her mother, an aspiring actress,
Davis once said, "I had to be the monster for both of us."
On-screen and off, the Oscar-winning leading lady lived up to the
self-description, fighting her studio at every turn (and winning)
and lending her domineering presence to a number of
"heavy" hall-of-famers (The Letter, Mr. Skeffington,
Beyond the Forest, Whatever Happened to Baby Jane?).

James Cagney (with Mae Clarke, right)
EACH DAWN I DIE, 1939 (ABOVE)
THE PUBLIC ENEMY, 1931 (RIGHT AND OVERLEAF)
*Having begun his show-biz career (incredibly) as a chorus girl
in a vaudeville revue, the former real-life Bowery boy was forever
typecast as a vicious hood or gun-toting gangster following his
chilling performance as a bootlegger-who-gets-too-big-for-his-boots
in the brutally uncompromising* The Public Enemy.
*(The infamous grapefruit scene caused women's groups around the
country to protest the on-screen abuse of Clarke.) A hoofer at heart,
the energetic star of* G-Men, Angels With Dirty Faces, *and*
Lady Killer *eventually got to showcase his considerable musical
talent in the Oscar-winning* Yankee Doodle Dandy.

Joan Crawford (with Barry Sullivan and Norma Shearer)
QUEEN BEE, 1955 (ABOVE)
THE WOMEN, 1939 (RIGHT)

*The former hard-luck shop girl born Lucille LeSueur rose through
hard work and sheer willpower to become MGM's biggest star of the
1930s and filmdom's most durable leading lady for over forty years.
Like the actress herself, Crawford's characters specialized in ruthlessly
climbing their way to the top. When her husband (Sullivan) in*
Queen Bee *and real- and reel-life nemesis (Shearer) in*
The Women *try to stop her, the queen's sting is poisonous indeed.*

Joan Crawford (with Wendell Corey)

HARRIET CRAIG, 1950

*Art imitated life in this cult classic based on the
George Kelly play about a perfectionist wife who will stop at
nothing to have her house and life run as she wants it.
With her close-cropped hair, and shoulders broader than ever,
Crawford gives an eerily convincing portrait of a domineering
housewife from hell. Crawford entered the real-life
"heavy" hall of fame when her adopted daughter Christina
alleged child abuse in* Mommie Dearest, *published
shortly after the star's death in 1977.*

Edward G. Robinson
LITTLE CAESAR, 1931
(LEFT AND OVERLEAF)
The movie that introduced a spate of 1930s
gangster flicks, this early talkie (based loosely
on the life of Al Capone) also made a star
of the bulldog-faced, thirty-seven-year-old
former Emmanuel Goldenberg in his role as
Rico Bandello. Typecast forever-after as the
archetypical gangster in films such as
The Sea Wolf *and* Key Largo, *the archvillain*
was in real life a gentle, cultivated man,
whose extensive art collection was one
of the world's finest.

21

John Malkovich
IN THE LINE OF FIRE, 1993 (ABOVE)

*Playing a particularly harrowing lunatic in this suspense thriller
starring Clint Eastwood, the character actor and sometime
screen villain dons a number of disguises as "Booth," an appropriately
nicknamed potential presidential assassin. Malkovich was another
kind of cad in his second-most-sinister role to date, as the sadistic
professional philanderer Valmont in* Dangerous Liaisons.

Alan Rickman (with Bonnie Bedelia)
DIE HARD, 1988 (RIGHT)

*The classically trained English actor is impeccably evil in this first of the
blockbuster action thrillers starring Bruce Willis. Garnering instant fame
as Hans Gruber, the suave international terrorist who commandeers an
L.A. office building, the late-blooming forty-two-year-old star has since
appeared in a number of Basil Rathbone-like roles, most appropriately as
the wicked Sheriff of Nottingham in* Robin Hood: Prince of Thieves.

Bruce Dern
BLACK SUNDAY, 1977

*A younger generation's Anthony Perkins,
the grandson of a former governor of Utah
and nephew of writer Archibald MacLeish
has created a memorable gallery of maniacs,
psychos, perverts, and creeps in films such as*
Hush . . . Hush . . . Sweet Charlotte,
Psych-Out, Will Penny, *and* Tattoo.
*Playing a flipped-out Vietnam vet who
pilots a killer blimp in this disaster thriller
directed by John Frankenheimer,
the multitalented Dern has only rarely
escaped his "Hollywood heavy" typecasting.*

Orson Welles (with Janet Leigh and Akim Tamiroff)
Touch of Evil, 1958 (above)
As the crooked cop Hank Quinlan, Welles is the heaviest
of the heavies in this seedy south-of-the-border tale of sex, drugs,
murder, and mayhem. Directed by the star himself and featuring
an all-star cast, the high-camp, low-budget cult classic is
one of the blackest portraits of evil ever captured on film—
a nasty nightmare from beginning to end.

Edward Arnold
(with James Stewart, Eugene Pallette, and Allan Cavan)
Mr. Smith Goes to Washington, 1939 (right)
The rotund real-life president of the Screen Actor's Guild played
a number of crooked heavies in over 150 films, including some
50 two-reelers made before 1920. Often cast as an uncompromising
politician or an amiable scoundrel, the one-time stage actor is perhaps
best known for his portrayal of the party boss who tries to steer
America's most civic-minded citizen wrong in this Frank Capra classic.

Ernest Borgnine (with Montgomery Clift)

FROM HERE TO ETERNITY, 1953

With his stout appearance, wild eyes, and gap teeth, the former stage and TV actor was a natural heavy. Garnering some acclaim for his first major role, as the sadistic Italian-hating sergeant "Fatso" in the celluloid version of James Jones's tawdry tale of army life, Borgnine seemed permanently typecast and went on to depict villains in Johnny Guitar *and* Bad Day at Black Rock. *In a daring role reversal, the actor next gave a sensitive portrayal of a lonely Brooklyn butcher in the low-budget sleeper* Marty, *winning a surprise Best Actor Oscar for his performance and stunning audiences with his overnight transformation from humdrum heavy to humble hero.*

Charles Middleton (with Beatrice Roberts)
FLASH GORDON, 1936
The most infamous of the 1930s fantasy-serial villains,
the one-time carnival and circus performer was a particularly ruthless
Ming the Merciless from the planet Mondo in this popular
Universal Studios feature based on the comic strip by Alex Raymond.
The definitive portrayal of extraterrestrial tyranny,
Middleton's malevolent master of the universe has been imitated
(but never equaled) by everyone from Max von Sydow in the campy
1980 remake to Peter Cushing in Star Wars.

Donald Pleasence and Honor Blackman (with Sean Connery)
You Only Live Twice, 1967 (above)
Goldfinger, 1964 (right)
With his unblinking blue eyes and feline fixation, Pleasence,
the British-born character actor and sinister star of numerous
international horror films, is a suitably sadistic Blofeld,
the never-before-seen archnemesis of Agent 007, in the last of the
James Bond spy-thriller installments to regularly feature
Sean Connery. A showcase for some of the screen's vilest-looking
villains, the series also featured some of its most fetching femmes
fatales, including Blackman as the judo-chopping Pussy Galore.

**Peter Lorre, Mary Astor, and Sydney Greenstreet
(with Humphrey Bogart)**

THE MALTESE FALCON, 1941

*The real-life scion of a prominent New York family was
ironically cast as a gangster in mostly B pictures before
landing his biggest break as the ruthless detective Sam
Spade in this classic thriller directed by John Huston.*

*Also introducing the dastardly duo of Lorre and
Greenstreet (in his first screen appearance), the Oscar-
nominated picture featured a new kind of tough guy—
half-heavy, half-hero—which Bogart parlayed with great
success in a number of seminal 1940s noir classics, including
Casablanca, To Have and Have Not, and Key Largo.
Hollywood's most celebrated celluloid cynic later reprised his
earlier hard-core heavy routine in films such as The Caine
Mutiny and The Desperate Hours, among others.*

Paul Muni (with Ann Dvorak)
SCARFACE, 1932 (ABOVE)

The forerunner of the Godfather *movies and the glossy 1983 remake, the Howard Hawks-directed masterpiece that turned the Hays office on its ear was the last in the spate of truly great gangster films that had begun the year before with* Little Caesar *and* The Public Enemy. *The title role in the Al Capone-based story of gaudy clothes, cars, and women made a star of the powerhouse graduate of New York's Yiddish theater, whose early Method-like acting technique made him Warner Bros.' most distinguished thespian and influenced a generation of antiheroes from Bogart to Brando.*

Wallace Beery
VIVA VILLA!, 1934 (RIGHT)

The gravel-voiced, rubbery-faced former husband of Gloria Swanson was adept at both comedy and villainy, having played a number of buffoons (occasionally in drag) and creeps throughout the silent era. With the advent of talkies, the actor demonstrated his unique versatility in more important ventures, ably playing the murderous Mexican bandito in Viva Villa! *and the hilariously gruff husband of Jean Harlow in* Dinner at Eight *in the same year.*

Gene Hackman
SUPERMAN, 1978 (ABOVE)

*The distinguished actor with the undistinguished face had played
a few memorable villains before his turn as the diabolical Lex Luthor
in* Superman. *Although he began his career late in life, Hackman
found success with his first heavy-with-a-heart part, as Warren
Beatty's brother in* Bonnie and Clyde, *and, later, as the hard-bitten
cop "Popeye" Doyle in* The French Connection.

Robert De Niro
CAPE FEAR, 1991 (RIGHT)

*De Niro transformed himself so completely into the psychopathic
Max Cady in this particularly gruesome Martin Scorsese remake of
the 1962 film, that critics and audiences were both thrilled and
appalled at the same time. Having played effective heavies previously
in* Mean Streets, The Godfather Part II, *and* Taxi Driver,
*the Method-trained Oscar winner created his most evil character
to date in a film that is depressingly devoid of heroes of any sort.*

Richard Kiel (with Roger Moore)
THE SPY WHO LOVED ME, 1977
The award for the biggest (and heaviest!) screen heavy of all time goes to the steel-toothed giant "Jaws" in this high-tech tenth installment of the James Bond spy series. The seven-feet-two-inch, 350-pound former nightclub bouncer with a 16EEE shoe size reprised his role as a killer thug-with-a-thyroid-problem in the film's follow-up, Moonraker.

Basil Rathbone (with Errol Flynn and Tyrone Power)

THE ADVENTURES OF ROBIN HOOD, 1938 (ABOVE)

THE MARK OF ZORRO, 1940 (RIGHT)

Gaunt, saturnine, and cerebral, the classically-trained British actor born Philip St. John Basil Rathbone made an ideal archenemy, crossing swords (he was Hollywood's most accomplished fencer) and exchanging quips with the big screen's leading heroes. Those qualities and the star's elegant English accent and haughty attitude made his villainous portrayals of the Sheriff of Nottingham and Zorro's nemesis Captain Pasquale (as well as Greta Garbo's husband in Anna Karenina *and the buccaneer in* Captain Blood*) all the more memorable. They also made him a convincingly cunning and aloof Sherlock Holmes, his most famous role, in fourteen films in the 1940s.*

Sir Laurence Olivier
MARATHON MAN, 1976 (ABOVE)

Nominated ten times for an Oscar (winning two) and arguably the greatest English-speaking actor of all time, Olivier made this otherwise standard-fare thriller something of a cause célèbre. Rarely called upon to play villains, the stunningly versatile Olivier gave a bone-chilling, teeth-chattering performance as the Nazi-dentist-with-a-killer-drill.

Lionel Barrymore (seated)
IT'S A WONDERFUL LIFE, 1946 (LEFT)

Another great actor who traded in his early starring roles for rich character parts in later life, the eldest and perhaps most talented of the celebrated acting clan lent his dominating presence to his role as the avaricious small-town banker in this beloved Frank Capra classic starring Jimmy Stewart. Although unable to stand or walk (Barrymore had been crippled since 1938), the actor still commanded the screen, his balefully malevolent performance upstaging everyone's but Stewart's.

Sharon Stone
BASIC INSTINCT, 1992 (ABOVE)

One of the first in the recent shock-'em-with-sex cycle of thriller pics, this blockbuster hit made a star of the former model and bit actress, who exposed more than just her talent as the Venus-flytrap villainess with a suspected penchant for ice picks. Bleached-blonde slick, Stone's sinister seductress is scary—but somehow not as sexy as the femmes fatales of an earlier era.

Glenn Close
FATAL ATTRACTION, 1987 (RIGHT)

Following her infamous role as that memorable frizzy-haired psychopath in Fatal Attraction, *Close won her place in the "heavy" hall of fame with her twisted turns as the game-playing Marquise de Merteuil in* Dangerous Liaisons *and the ice-queen heiress with an insulin problem in* Reversal of Fortune. *Not at all like her deranged-dame roles in real life, the Oscar-nominated actress is a sometime suburban housewife and professed Hollywood outsider.*

Lotte Lenya (above right, with Daniela Bianchi) and Grace Jones
FROM RUSSIA WITH LOVE, 1963 (ABOVE)
A VIEW TO A KILL (RIGHT)

Acted with tongues held firmly in cheek, the popular James Bond spy series has featured some of the big screen's most memorable villainesses with the even more memorable names (Honey, Pussy Galore, Domino, Plenty O'Toole, etc.). Particularly diabolical were two of the least comely: Lenya as Rosa Klebb, the KGB agent with a penchant for kicking people with her knife-equipped clodhopper shoes, and Jones as May Day, the muscle-bound bodyguard with a soft spot for 007. Wreaking havoc from the Soviet Union to the Silicon Valley, the two were every bit as evil as their killer-chick counterparts.

Richard Widmark (with Barbara Lawrence)
THE STREET WITH NO NAME, 1948 (ABOVE)

The durable actor garnered a Best Actor Oscar nomination his first time out, as the cackling psychopath in Kiss of Death. *Following up that chilling portrayal with an even more sinister depiction of a sadistic hood with a bad case of hypochondria in this documentary-style gangster film noir, Widmark eventually broadened his range to play the occasional hero, including his signature psycho-chasing cop in* Madigan.

James Mason (with Margaret Lockwood)
THE WICKED LADY, 1945 (RIGHT)

Cast early in his career as a romantic ruffian who brutalized women but always had them begging for more, the stage-trained Brit had the heroine doing just that in this heavy-handed costume drama that featured more daring décolletage than dastardly deeds. Arriving in Hollywood in the late 1940s, the workhorse actor eventually broke type and became one of the industry's most respected actors.

Humphrey Bogart
THE CAINE MUTINY, 1954 (ABOVE)
HIGH SIERRA, 1941 (RIGHT)

The grizzle-faced former B villain and real-life aristocrat born Humphrey DeForest Bogart eventually made his mark playing desperate men resigned to their own doom. Tough, cynical, but with a heart of gold, the actor's film-noir antiheroes had just enough soul to make them human. The "Bogey" legend ignited with his lead performance as Mad Dog Earle, the two-bit gangster going nowhere in High Sierra, *the late-blooming star made characters such as* Sam Spade (The Maltese Falcon), *Rick Blaine* (Casablanca), *Philip Marlowe* (The Big Sleep), *and Captain Queeg* (The Caine Mutiny) *instant Hollywood classics.*

Humphrey Bogart
(with Bette Davis and Leslie Howard)
THE PETRIFIED FOREST, 1936

His movie career having gone nowhere, Bogart got his
first acclaim on the stage playing Duke Mantee,
the John Dillinger-like gangster in this hit
Robert Sherwood play. When Warner Bros. later bought
the film rights and insisted on replacing B-actor Bogart
with Edward G. Robinson, Howard, the star of both
productions, threatened to quit. The gambit payed off,
landing the screen role for the lucky second lead,
who later named his first child by Lauren Bacall, Leslie,
in honor of the man who gave him his first big break.

Jack Palance (with Shelley Winters)
THE BIG KNIFE, 1955 (RIGHT)
SHANE, 1953 (OVERLEAF)

Nominated for Oscars over forty years ago for his cold-hearted villains in Sudden Fear *and* Shane, *the stage-trained coal miner's son with the gaunt, tight-skinned visage (the result of extensive plastic surgery after suffering severe burns in World War II) finally earned that prized award in 1991 for his outrageous comeback performance as "Curly" in the comedy hit* City Slickers. *Bringing to the role the mythic weight of over ninety years of westerns and his own heavy-hitting performances as the gun-toting tough in* Shane *and the shattered star-with-a-past in* The Big Knife, *Palance offered up brilliant Swanson-like self-parody that never lapsed into camp.*

Lee Van Cleef
THE GOOD, THE BAD, AND THE UGLY, 1967

With his sharp features and narrow, steely eyes, the New Jersey accountant-turned-cowboy was typecast as a sneaky villain in scores of mostly B westerns throughout the 1950s. Forsaking the Ponderosa for Palermo, the actor finally hit it big as "the bad" in Sergio Leone's seminal The Good *(Clint Eastwood),* the Bad, and the Ugly *(Eli Wallach), going on to box-office stardom as the cruel heavy in a number of big-budget spaghetti westerns.*

Christopher Walken

BATMAN RETURNS, 1992

*Beginning his career depicting more sensitive characters (winning
an early Oscar for his supporting role in* The Deer Hunter)*, the
fair-haired baker's son from Astoria, Queens, has specialized in
playing remote or haughty villains, from the gun-for-hire loner in*
Heaven's Gate *to the mercenary drug lord in* King of New York.
Playing on his high-camp cartoon creep in the James Bond thriller
A View to a Kill, *Walken's mega-millionaire meanie Max Shreck in
the hugely popular* Batman *sequel was a fittingly arch archenemy.*

Lee Marvin (with John Wayne and Gloria Grahame)
THE MAN WHO SHOT LIBERTY VALENCE, 1962 (ABOVE)
THE BIG HEAT, 1953 (RIGHT)

The toughest and roughest of the 1950s heavies, the tall, growling
former Marine specialized early on in stealing scenes with his
commanding presence, at his best throwing scalding coffee in Grahame's
face in his third picture, The Big Heat. *Soon after playing against a*
double-dose of Hollywood heroes (Wayne and Jimmy Stewart) as
Liberty Valence in John Ford's masterpiece, Marvin did an about-face,
portraying heroes with an only slightly-less-heavy hand. In the end,
the aging tough-guy won more notoriety from the landmark palimony
case waged against him than from any of his screen roles.

Walter Slezak
ONCE UPON A HONEYMOON, 1942 (ABOVE)
THE PIRATE, 1948 (RIGHT)

Playing the evil buccaneer in the Vincente Minnelli-directed cult musical The Pirate, *the rotund Austrian actor and sometime opera singer was cast as a menacing villain/bumbling idiot, a dual role the actor had perfected as the bungling Nazi husband of Ginger Rogers in his Hollywood debut,* Once Upon a Honeymoon. *Slezak later reprised his killer-Kraut routine (sans the bungling) for one of his best parts, as the sinister U-boat captain in the Alfred Hitchcock suspense masterpiece* Lifeboat.

Henry Daniell (with Errol Flynn)
THE SEA HAWK, 1940 (ABOVE)

*The cold-eyed, cynical British-born former stage actor was
one of Hollywood's most sought-after villains in the 1930s and 1940s,
playing both ruthless businessmen (the nasty tabloid editor in*
The Philadelphia Story*) and suave swashbucklers to great effect.
In the latter role, he shone blackly as the ambassador/spy
Lord Wolfingham who duels Flynn to the death in this* Robin Hood-
meets-Captain Blood *Warner Bros. classic.*

Vincent Price (with Barbara Bel Geddes)
THE LONG NIGHT, 1947 (RIGHT)

*Best remembered for his late-in-life incarnation as America's
aristocrat of evil, the Yale-educated, stage-trained actor and avid
art collector had begun his film career playing appropriately effete
villains. His performance as the creepy womanizer in this remake of
the French murder mystery,* Daybreak, *is a chilling foreboding
of his Roger Corman horror-cycle roles to come.*

Otto Preminger (with Joan Bennett)
STALAG 17, 1953 (ABOVE)
MARGIN FOR ERROR, 1943 (RIGHT)
No one played a more sinister Nazi than the bald-pated,
strutting Austrian-born director and sometime-actor (who
happened to be Jewish). Directing himself in his Hollywood acting
debut as the German goon in Margin for Error, *Preminger reprised*
a variation of that role for two more films, Pied Piper *and*
Billy Wilder's Oscar-winning Stalag 17. *His character in the*
latter was later the inspiration for the German commandant
in the hit TV series "Hogan's Heroes."

Tommy Lee Jones
UNDER SIEGE, 1992

Playing a deranged ex-Special Forces leader who takes over the USS Missouri *battleship and its crew, the talented and long-overlooked actor is the best thing about this big-box-office blood-and-guts actioner starring Steven Seagal. A versatile leading man, the rough-looking Texas-born star is at his best playing psychos and hard-headed heavies in films such as* The Eyes of Laura Mars, JFK, *and* The Fugitive. *Nominated for Academy Awards for the latter two, one of America's best actors is no longer one of its least known.*

Conrad Veidt (with Claude Rains)
THE THIEF OF BAGHDAD, 1940 (ABOVE)
CASABLANCA, 1942 (RIGHT)

Cool and cruel in his long, black robes as the evil grand vizier, the German film actor who rose to fame as the demonic Cesare in the silent masterpiece The Cabinet of Dr. Caligari *is a perfect archvillain in Alexander Korda's Technicolor fantasy based on* The Arabian Nights. *At one point detained from leaving Berlin by the Nazis, the world-famous star eventually escaped to Hollywood, where he was instantly typecast in an ironic succession of roles as scheming Nazis in films such as* Nazi Agent, Above Suspicion, *and* Casablanca, *his last picture.*

ATLANTIQUE
RABAT
FÈS
CASABLANCA
MOGADOR
MAROC
MARRAKECH
ERFOUD

Sylvester Stallone
(with Kate Murtagh, Robert Mitchum, and Joe Spinell)
FAREWELL, MY LOVELY, 1975

*Not all Hollywood heroes started out that way. The one-time bit
player born in New York City's Hell's Kitchen played a series of hoods
and heavies in mostly forgettable fare such as* Capone, Death Race
2000, *and this neo-film-noir sleeper featuring "heavy" hall-of-famer*
Mitchum. *The following year, the down-and-out actor became an*

Kathy Bates (with James Caan)

MISERY, 1990

*Proof that Hollywood really does love its heavies after all,
the little-known Bates stole the show from veteran actor Caan
and won a Best Actress Oscar for her harrowing performance
as the fanatical fan-gone-overboard in this grisly psycho-
thriller based on the novel by Stephen King.*

CREDITS AND SOURCES

TEXT: J. SPENCER BECK

DESIGN: LISA LYTTON-SMITH
PHOTO EDITOR: LESLIE FRATKIN

Front Cover: Everett Collection
3: Culver Pictures
6: Everett Collection
7: Photofest
9: Archive Photos
11: Courtesy The Kobal Collection
12: Everett Collection
13: Everett Collection
14-15: Culver Pictures
16: Photofest
17: Photofest
19: Photofest
20-21: Photofest
22-23: Culver Pictures
24: Everett Collection
25: Photofest
26-27: Everett Collection
28: Photofest
29: Everett Collection
31: Photofest
33: Photofest
34: Culver Pictures
35: Everett Collection
36-37: Archive Photos
38: Everett Collection
39: Photofest
40: Culver Pictures
41: Courtesy The Kobal Collection
42-43: Everett Collection
44: Archive Photos

45: Everett Collection
46-47: Photofest
47: Courtesy The Kobal Collection
48: Photofest
49: Photofest
50: Everett Collection
51: Culver Pictures
52: Photofest
53: Photofest
54: Lester Glassner Collection/Neal Peters
55: Neal Peters Collection
56-57: Courtesy The Kobal Collection
59: Lester Glassner Collection/Neal Peters
60-61: Lester Glassner Collection/Neal Peters
62: Photofest
63: Photofest
64: Photofest
65: Lester Glassner Collection/Neal Peters
66: Photofest
67: Photofest
68: Everett Collection
69: Culver Pictures
70: Photofest
71: Photofest
72-73: Everett Collection
74: Photofest
75: Culver Pictures
76-77: Everett Collection
78: Everett Collection
Back Cover: Courtesy The Kobal Collection